What Are the Sacraments?

Crucial Questions booklets provide a quick introduction to definitive Christian truths. This expanding collection includes titles such as:

Who Is Jesus?

Can I Trust the Bible?

Does Prayer Change Things?

Can I Know God's Will?

How Should I Live in This World?

What Does It Mean to Be Born Again?

Can I Be Sure I'm Saved?

What Is Faith?

What Can I Do with My Guilt?

What Is the Trinity?

TO BROWSE THE REST OF THE SERIES,
PLEASE VISIT: **LIGONIER.ORG/CQ**

CQ

What Are the Sacraments?

R.C. SPROUL

 LIGONIER MINISTRIES

What Are the Sacraments?
© 2023 by the R.C. Sproul Trust

Published by Ligonier Ministries
421 Ligonier Court, Sanford, FL 32771
Ligonier.org

Printed in China
RR Donnelley
0001122
First edition

ISBN 978-1-64289-437-0 (Paperback)
ISBN 978-1-64289-438-7 (ePub)
ISBN 978-1-64289-439-4 (Kindle)

Cover design: Ligonier Creative
Interior typeset: Katherine Lloyd, The DESK

Ligonier Ministries edited and adapted Dr. R.C. Sproul's original material to create this volume. We are thankful to Mrs. Vesta Sproul for her invaluable help on this project.

Scripture quotations are from the ESV® Bible (The Holy Bible, English Standard Version®), copyright © 2001 by Crossway, a publishing ministry of Good News Publishers. Used by permission. All rights reserved.

Library of Congress Control Number: 2022930840

Contents

Chapter One

What Is a Sacrament?

Throughout church history, there have been perhaps few issues that have led to as many disputes as the sacraments. We've seen debates over how many sacraments there are, how these sacraments operate, how they are to be performed, who is to receive them, and so on. There has been much confusion and conflict. Although we can't go into minute detail here about all the technical theological points involved with the sacraments, we can look at some of the basic principles.

We understand that the life and worship of the church involve what we call *Word and sacrament*. Our churches—Protestant churches, particularly—have emphasized the preaching of the Word, whereas churches in the Middle Ages tended to feature the celebration of the Lord's Supper; this is why the centerpiece of church architecture was the altar. Many Protestant churches instead made the pulpit the point of focus, emphasizing preaching rather than sacraments. Sometimes we tend to overreact in one direction or the other. But from the days of the Old Testament all the way through the New Testament, God has been concerned not only to speak to His people through His Word but also to communicate in other ways, including through the sacraments.

The English word *sacrament* comes from the Latin *sacramentum*, which is a translation of the Greek word *mystērion*. Our English Bibles translate the Greek as "mystery." Historically, the church saw that something mysterious was involved in the liturgy of the church and in the giving of sacraments. So right from the start, we find a bit of difficulty as we try to define what a sacrament is. But in its most rudimentary form, the idea of the sacrament involves an experience of something that is *sacred*—something that we regard as extraordinary or uncommon, something with a special meaning or significance attached to it.

Theologians sometimes use the word *sacrament* in a narrow sense and sometimes in a broad sense. In the narrow sense, the term means the specific rites or ordinances that are observed in the church, which we call *sacraments*. In the broader sense, it refers to the many ways that God communicates to His people through object lessons, signs, or ordinary symbols that take on extraordinary meaning.

For example, early in the Old Testament, we have the record of the great deluge, the flood of Noah that destroyed the world. We know that after Noah and his family survived, God promised them that He would never again destroy the world by a flood. We are told that as a sign or symbol of God's abiding promise to that end, God set His rainbow in the sky. He used the common, natural phenomenon of the rainbow as a sign of an uncommon, special, divine promise of His persevering and preserving providence. So every time we see a rainbow, we are involved in the sacramental life of the faith—not in the narrow, technical sense of sacraments but rather in the broader sense of external objects that are used to enhance and support the communication of the verbal promises of God.

In the Old Testament, God ordained several rites as sureties of His promise. For instance, He gave Israel the sign of circumcision, which had symbolic meaning to the people (see Gen. 17). He made a covenant with Abraham in which, in a dream, God Himself appeared in a theophany (a visible manifestation of God) as a torch moving between the torn pieces of animals that God had instructed Abraham to cut in half (see Gen. 15). God was essentially saying, "I'm demonstrating the certainty of the promise of My word." God's verbal promise was upheld by the nonverbal visible sign that accompanies it. The Old Testament prophets frequently used object lessons, dramatizing the word of God with a visual apparatus or sign, such as a plumb line (Amos 7) or a broken jar (Jer. 19). The idea here is taking something that is common and ordinary and using it for extraordinary, uncommon ways of giving testimony to the truth of God.

Anthropologists have studied the religious behavior of people around the world, not only in Christian environments but also in other environments such as Jewish, Hindu, Shinto, Confucian, and Muslim. They have found that all people groups that engage in religious practices, no matter what religion they're committed to, have some concept of sacrament, or at least some concept of what we call *sacred space* or *sacred time*. Again, we find examples in the pages of the Old Testament. When Noah landed safely after the flood, what did he do? He marked the spot; he built an altar (see Gen. 8). After Jacob had his midnight dream at Bethel, he took the rock on which he had rested during the night, anointed it with oil, and named that place the House of God, because there God had appeared to him (see Gen. 28). We think, for example, of Moses' encounter with God in the burning bush in the Midianite wilderness. God commanded Moses: "Moses, Moses! . . . Take your sandals off your feet, for the place on which you are standing is holy ground" (Ex. 3:4–5). Holy ground is ground that is now uncommon, extraordinary, filled with meaning and significance, because there an intersection took place between the divine and the human, between the Creator and the creature. God met with Moses on that spot, and so that spot became holy ground. That's what we mean by *sacred space*.

My wife and I and our children and their spouses once took a trip to England, where we visited Stonehenge. To this day, nobody knows for sure how those big rocks got there and what their use was. Was it a religious thing? An astronomical thing? Experts still debate it, but the consensus is that Stonehenge was associated with religion and that it became a sacred site, a sacred place. Some of us have visited Jerusalem, a city that we call the Holy City. We sing a song, "I walked today where Jesus walked." There is something uncanny, almost eerie about visiting those places in this world where there was the meeting between heaven and earth. We have a sense of awe as we walk over the stones of the road to Emmaus or on the Via Dolorosa where Jesus walked to His crucifixion.

Now, the Bible doesn't authorize any sacralization of those stones or those streets. But that's part of our common response as human beings. When you were a child and you were distressed for some reason or another, perhaps you had a favorite place that you went for solace or for comfort, a place you sought when you wanted to be alone—in a tree house or in a closet or in your bedroom—someplace that had special significance to you. Part of our human experience is taking that which is ordinary and imbuing it with special significance because of its association with something transcendent, something supremely important.

We see that human practice developing throughout the pages of Scripture. For instance, there is the Old

Testament celebration of the Passover. The Passover was a key redemptive-historical event in the life of Israel, when God, in liberating His people from slavery in Egypt, caused His judgment to fall on Pharaoh and the Egyptians, so that God slew the firstborn son of every Egyptian family, including the son of Pharaoh. God had instructed His people to mark the doorposts of their houses with the blood of a lamb, the Passover lamb, so that when the angel of death came to the land and saw that a house was marked with the blood of the lamb, the angel of death passed over and the children of Israel were spared. Immediately after this event, they were liberated by the exodus.

In the history of Israel, the exodus stands as an event of paramount importance. So God instituted an annual celebration—the Passover feast for His people. He gave explicit instructions on how the Passover was to be observed—the specific food and wine that were to be used at this meal and the discussion that was to take place. It was not simply an empty celebration; the sacrament was also wedded to the Word. God essentially said: "Every year unto all generations at this time, you are to gather and celebrate this event. When your children ask you, 'Why are we doing this?' you will tell them how I rescued you from bondage and how I spared you from judgment in the Passover" (see Ex. 12:24–27). This became deeply rooted in the religion of Israel. It became so important to Israel that shortly before the death of Christ Jesus, as He entered into His passion and began to feel the initial pangs of His torment, He said that He earnestly desired to celebrate the Passover one more time with His disciples before He left this world (Luke 22:15). That meal celebrates not just a place but a *sacred time*.

We have moments in our lives that we say were formative in the shaping of our lives. We celebrate birthdays every year. We celebrate Good Friday, Easter, Christmas—observances not commanded in the Scriptures. The Bible doesn't say that we're supposed to celebrate Easter or Christmas, and some Christians protest the celebration of those events for one reason or another. The reason, however, that the church celebrates those specific occasions is that they mark, in our memory, sacred time. Good Friday was the day on which our Savior died, on which the atonement was made—the most important day in human history. Then we mark the day of resurrection. We mark the day of Christ's birth, the day of His ascension, and the day of Pentecost. These are not sacraments in the narrow, technical sense, but they are sacramental in the broad and general sense in which I'm speaking because they involve an observation of sacred space and sacred time. In one single word, these places and times are regarded as *holy*. The term *holy* chiefly refers to that which is *other* or different, that which is uncommon, that which rises above the normal and the mundane. I believe we miss something in the life of the church and in the life of the Christian if we fail to understand the deep significance of these historic moments, places, and signs.

For example, consider the Lord's Supper. On the night on which He was betrayed, Jesus took the Old Testament sacrament of Passover and filled it with new meaning and new content, saying, "This is my blood of the covenant, which is poured out for many for the forgiveness of sins" (Matt. 26:28). He attached a new significance to an ancient rite. At this point, the bread no longer represented the unleavened bread that was eaten in haste as the people were preparing to leave Egypt and go to the promised land; instead, it symbolized the body of Christ. "This is my body, which is given for you," He declared in the midst of that feast (Luke 22:19).

We will look briefly at some of the differences that Christians have in their understanding of the meaning of the Lord's Supper. But for now, let us remember that Jesus instituted this sacrament, and that He did so in the middle of participating in the old sacrament. He did it for much the same reason that the ancient nation of Israel did. He said, "Do this in remembrance of me" (Luke 22:19). Jesus knew His people. He knew that sometimes our faithfulness is only as strong as our recollection of our most recent blessing at the hands of God. But we come down from those mountaintop experiences, and we tend to forget what God has done for us in the past. We tend to want to live from blessing to blessing, always needing to be replenished with the assurance that God is with us. I think that the disciples could have forgotten many things that they learned from Jesus—His teachings, His example. It is as though Jesus said: "Whatever else you might forget, don't forget what's going to happen tomorrow. Don't ever forget My death. I want to seal this into your memories forever, so that as often as you eat of this food and drink of this cup, you show forth My death until I come." So from that point on, the Lord instituted a special ceremony, a special event, to commemorate the most sacred time that God had wrought in human history.

Chapter Two

How Many Sacraments?

G od has given us not only His Word but also external
signs and symbols by which He confirms the words of
His promises, demonstrates to us vitally important elements
of truth, and commands that certain events and occasions be
remembered by every generation. There is a collective memory in the life of the church for which God is concerned,
and this involves the practice and use of the sacraments.

One of the first questions that arises in any discussion of
the sacraments concerns the *number* of sacraments. We do

not have universal agreement on that subject. The Roman Catholic Church designates seven sacraments, which we'll look at in a moment. The majority of Protestant bodies recognize two sacraments, but some recognize three, and some deny the idea of sacrament altogether. A former seminary student of mine was a member of a communion that didn't believe in sacraments at all. One day in class we were discussing the Lord's Supper, and this student asked, "Why does it matter whether we have bread and wine at communion or if we just come together and enjoy Coca-Cola and peanut-butter-and-jelly sandwiches?" I replied, somewhat sharply, "It matters because Jesus didn't consecrate peanut-butter-and-jelly sandwiches and Coca-Cola."

Our discussion in that class was on the proper means of the sacrament. Do we use the things that are common, such as bread and wine, or can we substitute whatever we want for them? The point I was trying to make is that the reason that these particular elements are used and not others is that these are the elements that Christ instituted, and that's the way God ordained for the sacraments to be observed.

Behind that student's question was a broader question: Where do sacraments come from? My response to the student was based on the classic Protestant argument for limiting the sacraments to two, which is that two and only two sacraments were directly and explicitly instituted by Christ. This takes us back to the sixteenth-century debate over the number of the sacraments.

Historically, in the development of the Roman Catholic Church, Rome came to the conclusion that there are seven sacraments of the church, including baptism and the Lord's Supper (or the Eucharist). In addition to those two, Roman Catholicism has five other sacraments: confirmation, penance or reconciliation, anointing of the sick or extreme unction, matrimony, and holy orders. Thomas Aquinas, in defending this number, argued that these are special divine signs and conduits of special grace meant to assist human beings in all the major transitions and moments of their lives.

For the Roman Catholic Church, there are three sacraments that are considered sacraments of initiation. First is the sacrament of baptism, which is given at the beginning of life. An initial grace of salvation is bestowed on the infant in the child's baptism, according to Rome, and the child then receives an indelible sign or mark of his being cleansed from original sin. (We'll look more closely at this later when we study the content of the sacraments of baptism and the Lord's Supper.) Rome sees baptism as an initial means of grace.

Next—though the order has varied over the course of Roman Catholic history—comes confirmation. When children reach the "age of discretion" or the "age of reason"—at which time they are considered morally responsible for their actions—they undergo catechetical instruction and are then able to profess faith for themselves. Through the sacrament of confirmation, they become full members of the church.

Historically, confirmation precedes and admits a child to the final sacrament of initiation, the Eucharist or Lord's Supper. This sacrament is provided for the ongoing sanctifying and strengthening of the soul in the Christian life.

There are two sacraments that are considered sacraments of healing. First, the sacrament of penance or reconciliation, which includes confession, has always been important in the Roman Catholic Church. It is a sacrament of spiritual healing, and the church describes it as the "second plank of justification" for those who have made "shipwreck of their faith." That is, when a person is baptized, he receives an infusion of saving grace, the grace of justification, and the child remains in a state of grace until or unless he commits a mortal sin. Mortal sin is called *mortal* because it has the ability to kill that saving grace that is in a person's soul. Once the person has destroyed his salvation, he needs to be restored into a state of grace. The means of that restoration is through the sacrament of penance.

Then there is the sacrament of the anointing of the sick, also known as extreme unction. It is a sacrament of physical healing—based on James 5:14–15: "Is anyone among you sick? Let him call for the elders of the church, and let them pray over him, anointing him with oil in the name of the Lord. And the prayer of faith will save the one who is sick"—though nowadays it is often restricted to those who are near death. In this use, it is sometimes called "last rites," though that term properly refers not only to the anointing of the sick but also to penance and the Eucharist, which would grant the recipient a final anointing of grace in preparation for death.

There are two sacraments that grant entrance into special states in the Roman Catholic Church. The first is the sacrament of matrimony. As Thomas Aquinas said, added grace is given to help sustain this closest of all human relationships. A good marriage is one that depends on the grace of God for strength and nurture.

Next is the sacrament of holy orders. This sacrament has to do with the ordination of a person to the priesthood, which is seen as an occasion when special grace is given to the person being ordained. He is then empowered and authorized to perform the Mass, to administer the sacraments, and to preach the Word, among other things.

It is interesting that the debate over the number of sacraments continues. Most Protestant churches do not see confirmation as a sacrament, but many Protestant churches nevertheless practice confirmation. That is, part of the special liturgy of the life of the church is a rite that marks a significant moment in a child's development: becoming fully included in the visible church. Likewise, in virtually every church, matrimony is seen as a sacred rite, a sacred covenant, a sacred ordinance. Even though it's technically not regarded as or called a *sacrament* in most churches, it is a special occasion. We don't have penance in most Protestant churches, though many have a time of corporate confession of sin as part of their liturgy. Martin Luther, for example, wanted to keep some of the elements of this rite in the life of the church while eliminating some of the things he objected to in the original sacrament of penance. Likewise, though we don't call it "holy orders," most Protestant churches have some kind of special rite for ordination of church officers who are set apart for service. Similarly, most churches do not have a formal rite of extreme unction, but many Protestant churches have healing services, in which people are anointed with oil, following James 5. A common practice, too, is the ministerial visitation of those who are dying, in which one prays with those who are in extreme situations to prepare them for the end of their lives.

With so many similar rites, why does one group call them *sacraments* and another doesn't? The basic reason, historically, is how one understands the *nature* of a sacrament and how one understands the *institution* of the sacrament. The Roman Catholic Church, for example, would say that Jesus instituted extreme unction. He didn't do it personally during His earthly ministry, but He did it vicariously or indirectly through the mandate of James, whose Apostolic word is considered an extension of the word of Christ. Likewise, Jesus didn't directly set apart marriage as a sacrament, yet He sanctified the event of marriage by His presence at the wedding feast of Cana. Do you see the difference between *directly instituting* and *indirectly sanctioning*? Much of the debate centers on this point. The Protestant tradition, which tends to be more narrow, says that a sacrament is a sacrament only if there is an explicit, direct institution or mandate by Jesus in the New Testament. That's why Protestantism restricts the number of sacraments to two.

Things become even more difficult when we find that there are things that Jesus seems to institute in the New Testament that don't appear even in the seven sacraments of Rome or in most of the sacramental theology of the church. Some Christian churches practice foot washing, for example, because Christ gave the example of foot washing and commanded His disciples to wash one another's feet. The bottom line is that there is no universal agreement on how many sacraments we should have in the church and on the ultimate distinction between a rite, an ordinance, and a sacrament.

In the Old Testament, special significance was assigned to circumcision and to the Passover. Those were clearly commanded by God. But they weren't the only activities He commanded to Old Testament Israel. Feasts and festivals were to be carried out with great religious significance, such as the Feast of Weeks and the Feast of Tabernacles. The Day of Atonement was practiced annually in Israel until it was fulfilled in the New Testament. So there's nothing magical about the specific number that we assign to these things. What we really want is to experience the full measure of God's grace and God's help for His people in the life of the church.

It is a great danger in our day to divorce Word and sacrament. The Word and the sacraments should go together. We want to avoid the problem of *sacramentalism*, in which people begin to put their trust and confidence in the working of the sacraments rather than in the promises of God that are the verbal part of the gospel. Those who minimize the Word and maximize the sacraments are *sacramentalists*. But sometimes in our attempt to correct that abuse, we neglect the sacraments. Some people point to the Old Testament prophets who criticized the rituals and rites of the Jews, but they did not attack the rites themselves, only the misuse of them. In the history of the Bible, we have both the verbal Word and the nonverbal dramatization of that Word through the sacraments and associated signs.

In the remaining chapters, we will be specifically looking at the two sacraments—baptism and the Lord's Supper.

Growing up in a Protestant community, I confess that the sacraments didn't mean much to me. I didn't know the significance of the rituals. But after I became a Christian, I studied the Scriptures and theology, and I began to learn the meaning of baptism and the Lord's Supper. The sacraments then became extremely important to me. I love the Word, but I also love the dramatization of the Word in the sacraments. We often fail to enjoy or discover and experience the fullness of the sacraments because we don't know what they mean. That's where I'm hoping our brief study will help.

Chapter Three

The Baptism of John

Very early in the Gospel accounts, we encounter baptism in the work of John the Baptist. It's important to understand John's baptism for several reasons. First, we have to understand that what we know as New Testament baptism—the baptism that Christ instituted and commanded His Apostles to administer to disciples in all nations in the name of the Father and the Son and the Holy Ghost—was *not* what John was performing. The baptism of John the Baptist is linked to the baptism of Christ and the baptism of the New Testament. But baptism as instituted by Jesus was a sign of the new covenant. Just as in the Old Testament the sign of the covenant was circumcision, so the sign of the covenant in the New Testament was baptism. John carried out his ministry before the new covenant was inaugurated and initiated by Jesus.

Jesus said, "The Law and the Prophets were until John" (Luke 16:16). That word "until" in the Greek means "up to and including"; John belongs to the Old Testament economy. That is an important point to understand because we can become confused when we read about the life and ministry of John the Baptist in the New Testament; we don't read about him in the Old Testament. The New Testament is called the book of the new covenant, but not everything that is contained in the pages of the New Testament refers to the period of the new covenant that was instituted by Christ in the upper room at the end of His life. This is important for understanding not only John the Baptist's ministry but also Jesus' earthly life and ministry. Jesus in His earthly life was required to fulfill all the requirements that God had laid on Israel in the old covenant. So the new covenant does not begin on the first page of the New Testament.

We meet this somewhat mysterious figure, John the Baptist, in the initial pages of the New Testament. Matthew writes:

In those days John the Baptist came preaching in the wilderness of Judea, "Repent, for the kingdom of heaven is at hand." For this is he who was spoken of by the prophet Isaiah when he said,

"The voice of one crying in the wilderness:
'Prepare the way of the Lord;
make his paths straight.'"

Now John wore a garment of camel's hair and a leather belt around his waist, and his food was locusts and wild honey. Then Jerusalem and all Judea and all the region about the Jordan were going out to him, and they were baptized by him in the river Jordan, confessing their sins.

But when he saw many of the Pharisees and Sadducees coming to his baptism, he said to them, "You brood of vipers! Who warned you to flee from the wrath to come? Bear fruit in keeping with repentance. And do not presume to say to yourselves,

'We have Abraham as our father,' for I tell you, God is able from these stones to raise up children for Abraham. Even now the axe is laid to the root of the trees. Every tree therefore that does not bear good fruit is cut down and thrown into the fire.

"I baptize you with water for repentance, but he who is coming after me is mightier than I, whose sandals I am not worthy to carry. He will baptize you with the Holy Spirit and fire. His winnowing fork is in his hand, and he will clear his threshing floor and gather his wheat into the barn, but the chaff he will burn with unquenchable fire." (Matt. 3:1–12)

Matthew makes a distinction between the ministry of John and the ministry of Jesus who was to come, and between the baptism of John and the baptism that Jesus will perform after He begins His public ministry. We also notice that when Matthew introduces John, he appeals to an Old Testament text that prophesied the coming of one who would be the forerunner of the Messiah, the one who was called to prepare the way of the Lord and to make His paths straight (see Isa. 40:3). The Gospel writers identify John the Baptist as the person who fulfilled that Old Testament prophecy of the one who would prepare the way for the Messiah. So the first thing that we have to understand about John the Baptist is that his ministry was a preparatory ministry; he was preparing the people of Israel for the coming of their long-awaited and promised Messiah.

John's baptism was somewhat of a scandal to the religious authorities of his day. Matthew tells us that he came out of the wilderness of Judea with a simple message: "Repent, for the kingdom of heaven is at hand" (Matt. 3:2). John called Israel to submit to this practice of baptism, which he performed at the Jordan River. Matthew records that people from Jerusalem and Judea and from all over the countryside flocked to the banks of the Jordan to submit to the baptism of John, but the Pharisees and the Sadducees, the religious leaders of the day, would not submit to this ritual and were quite offended by it. Why were they so scandalized by John's ministry?

It's important to remember that the Old Testament canon had been closed and that no prophet had arisen in Israel for four hundred years. The last canonical prophet had been Malachi, whose final prophecy predicted the return of Elijah as the one who would prepare the way of the coming Messiah (Mal. 4:5–6). We also know that in a somewhat cryptic way, Jesus identified John the Baptist with this promised Elijah who was to come (see Matt. 11:13–14).

The practice of baptism as John performed it did have historical roots in the early religious life of Israel. Before John, there emerged in the religion of the people of Israel the practice of what is called *proselyte baptism*. A *proselyte* is a convert to a particular religion. When people are engaged in evangelism, it is sometimes said that they are *proselytizing* others. That is, they are seeking the conversion of people to a given faith. In the Old Testament world, if a gentile converted as a proselyte to the covenant faith of Israel, he was required to take certain steps before he could be a full member of the community of Israel. First, the person had to embrace and profess the content of the faith of the Old Testament religion. Second, a male had to submit to the rite of circumcision, which was the sign of Old Testament religion. And third, the person had to undergo proselyte baptism.

The function of proselyte baptism was to communicate a symbolic rite or liturgy of cleansing and purification. Remember that gentiles in the Old Testament economy were considered to be foreigners to the covenant of Israel, and they were also considered to be unclean. So if a non-Jew, a gentile, wanted to convert to Judaism in the Old Testament, he had to take a bath, so to speak; he had to go through a purification ritual so that he would be made clean and consecrated and then be ready to become a full member of the household of Israel. In the New Testament, particularly in the book of Acts, we read about a particular group called God-fearers. Cornelius was numbered among the God-fearers; we remember the incident of Peter at Cornelius' house (Acts 10). God-fearers were people, usually from the Greek world, who converted to Israel in terms of embracing the faith of Israel. But they did not become full-fledged members of the commonwealth of Israel because they declined to go through the rite of adult circumcision. We can understand why grown men would have some reluctance to submit to that particular ritual. They said, "We embrace the faith; we fear the God of Israel, we worship Him, and we are Jews in every respect, except that we have not submitted to circumcision." That class of people were called the *God-fearers*. Those who did convert all the way, insofar as accepting the rite of circumcision, were also required to take a purification, cleansing bath, which was called proselyte baptism.

After four hundred years of silence from canonical prophets, this fellow, John the Baptist, emerges from the wilderness dressed very much like the prophet Elijah in the Old Testament—and the desert or the wilderness was the traditional place of meeting between God and His prophets. John behaves like an Old Testament prophet and preaches like an Old Testament prophet, but his message is somewhat different. In the Old Testament, the prophets spoke about the coming of the Messiah in the future, at an unknown, unspecified time. Sometime in the future, the Messiah would come. John's message is much more urgent, however; he comes declaring that the kingdom of heaven is at hand, that the axe is laid at the root of the tree, that His winnowing fork is in His hand—and this represents a period of crisis for Israel. As the herald of the Messiah, John announces that the Messiah is coming after him and that He's coming quickly after him; He's ready to appear at any moment on the scene.

John announces Jesus as "the Lamb of God, who takes away the sin of the world" (John 1:29). He announces Jesus as the One who was to come, and he even baptizes Jesus, which raises all kinds of questions. This was scandalous to the Pharisees and the Sadducees. Never before had

Jews been called to submit to baptism. This was an innovation by John the Baptist, one that would be repugnant to the orthodox religious leaders of the day, because the only one who would have the authority to institute such a radically new program would be an authentic prophet—it would require nothing less than the authority of the word of God to do it.

That's why John's role as a prophet is so important; he is delivering a new word to Israel, a new requirement. He is proclaiming: "In this moment of crisis, when the Messiah is about to appear, everybody in Israel has to take a bath. Everybody in Israel is now not clean enough or pure enough to meet the awaited Messiah, and so a requirement that had previously been limited to gentiles is now levied to Jews." That's why, when the Pharisees objected to this, they objected to it on the grounds that they were the children of Abraham. They were saying: "We are the seed of Abraham; we are the circumcised descendants of Abraham; we are the heirs of the covenant promises of God. We don't need to behave like converted gentiles; we don't need a bath." John the Baptist replied: "God can raise up children of Abraham from these stones. God is now requiring all of Israel to submit to this rite of cleansing."

Jesus willingly came forward, presented Himself to John at the Jordan, and told John to baptize Him. John's response was extreme reluctance: "Wait a minute. I can't baptize You. You should be baptizing me, because for the Lamb-without-blemish to be baptized would be for the Lamb-without-blemish to indicate that He has a blemish, that He is dirty, that He needs to be cleansed from His sin. If the Messiah is One who needs to repent, then He can't really qualify to be the Messiah." We feel the weight of this drama that took place. Jesus said to John, "Let it be so now, for thus it is fitting for us to fulfill all righteousness" (Matt. 3:15). Jesus commanded John to baptize Him, not because Jesus was saying, "I am a sinner and I need to be clean," but because Jesus, as the Messiah of Israel, became the representative of the nation. And as part of His messianic vocation, Jesus was required to fulfill every jot and tittle of the Old Testament law. He had to do this for His people.

If God requires this new work of baptism of the nation, and the Messiah is to fulfill the requirements in Himself for the nation, then Jesus has to submit to baptism—not as a sign of the cleansing of His own sin, but as a sign of the cleansing of the sins of the people whom He is representing. What is going on here is a special work of preparation at a special time in redemptive history, the time of the inauguration of the kingdom of God, the time of the breakthrough of the King, the Messiah who is coming. The baptism of John the Baptist was principally designed to prepare Israel for the coming of Jesus. So we see that it is not the same baptism that Jesus institutes as a sign of those who are now being embraced in the covenant community of the New Testament. Now every believer in the New Testament is required to be baptized. Baptism takes on a richer significance and broader application once it is instituted by Christ than the restricted significance it had during the ministry of John the Baptist.

The main thing we need to remember about the ministry of preparatory baptism in the work of John the Baptist is that baptism for John and later in the teaching of Jesus involves the sign of cleansing from sin. Though we may not all be of Jewish descent, we all come into the presence of God marred by sin, and we are all unclean. And so the work of baptism, both in the case of John and in the case of Jesus, clearly serves to communicate that important reality to us—that water is used for cleansing. The chief perspective of baptism is with a view to cleansing—not our clothes, but our souls—from the stain that we have from our sin.

Chapter Four

The Significance of Baptism

What is baptism? What is its significance? The word *significance* has a smaller word contained within it: *sign*. One of the ways that sacraments have historically been defined is as outward signs for inward grace. They are signs of something. A sign is something that points beyond itself to something else. If baptism is a sign, to what is it pointing? What is it signifying? What is its significance?

First, we see that baptism is the covenant sign of the New Testament. It is a sign that points to a person's relationship to a covenant. In the Old Testament, the sign of the covenant in Israel was circumcision, and circumcision had both a positive and a negative meaning. Positively, removing the foreskin signified that God was cutting apart or setting apart Israel from the rest of the world and that Israel was God's chosen nation, His holy seed, His royal priesthood. God entered into a covenant with the Jewish people and became their covenant Lord. This covenant had certain stipulations, and those who entered into this special agreement with Yahweh, the Lord God, confirmed their allegiance to God graphically, dramatically, and irreversibly by the rite of circumcision. The positive significance of that sign was that they were being set apart or consecrated, cut out from among the rest of the people in the pagan world.

The sign also had a negative significance. By swearing his oath to the covenant treaty with God, a Jew was saying by this sign: "God, if I fail to regard Your law, if I fail to keep the terms of this covenant, may I be cut off from You. May I be cut off from Your presence and from Your grace, just as I have cut off the foreskin of my flesh." The sign of circumcision at a human level was a reflection of what God had done at a divine level when He swore His promise to Abraham in Genesis 15.

In his nighttime vision, Abraham sees a smoking firepot and a torch pass between pieces of animals that had been cut in half according to God's direction. In this vision, God is represented by the flame that passes between the pieces of the animals. God is swearing His allegiance to the covenant and saying to Abraham, "Abraham, if I fail to keep My promises in this covenant, may I be torn apart, may I be cut in half, just as you have cut these animals in half." Even God, in a transcendent way, is, as it were, circumcised as the sign of His promise to stand behind the terms of the covenant.

Throughout the Old Testament, this sign of the covenant promises of God was repeated from generation to generation. And though New Testament baptism differs in some significant ways from circumcision, one of the things that baptism has in common with circumcision is that it is a covenant sign. It is the sign of the new covenant made for us in Christ.

Baptism is also significant because it is a sign of spiritual regeneration. What is the point of regeneration? To be reborn or regenerated in New Testament terms is to be made alive spiritually by God and by the power of the Holy Spirit and, in this process, to be delivered from the bondage of original sin. So regeneration is the work of God, by which God the Holy Spirit changes our hearts of stone to hearts of flesh and quickens us unto spiritual life. Regeneration is a resurrection from spiritual death, and in this process, we are cleansed, as it were, from the stain of original sin. Baptism, in using water much as the basin in the Old Testament tabernacle and temple did, points to our need for cleansing and signifies our being cleansed from original sin through the Spirit's work of divine regeneration.

Baptism also signifies our adoption into the family of God. Those who are adopted into God's family are given an outward mark, an outward sign, of their being engrafted into Christ, because that's how we are adopted. Christ and Christ alone is the natural Son of God, the eternal Son of God. We are "by nature children of wrath" (Eph. 2:3). We are not born into the family of God; we are not born into the kingdom of God. We must be reborn into the kingdom of God. Those who are reborn are also engrafted into Christ and, being engrafted into Christ, are therefore adopted into the family of God. The metaphor of adoption is used again and again in the New Testament to describe our relationship to God our Father. The family seal or mark of our adoption and of our being engrafted into Christ is baptism; it is the sign of the covenant, which includes our adoption into the family of God.

Baptism also signifies the believer's participation in the death and resurrection of Christ. To put it another way, baptism signifies our participation in the humiliation and exaltation of Christ. That's why Paul frequently labors the point that those who refuse to participate in the suffering and humiliation of Christ will not participate in the resurrection and exaltation of Christ. Baptism marks our engrafting to Jesus, our identifying ourselves with Christ, and that means that we now identify with His suffering and exaltation.

Baptism is also a sign of our sanctification and of our justification. You cannot be sanctified unless you are first justified, and you can't be adopted unless you are first justified. Now, all these different things for which baptism is a sign are really different facets of the same thing. Baptism is a sign of our salvation.

We recall from the previous chapter that John the Baptist announced that the One who would come after him would baptize with the Holy Spirit. Today there is a lot of controversy about the difference between water baptism and Spirit baptism, and certainly there is a difference. We can administer the sign of the new covenant and baptize people in water, but no one has the power or authority to baptize anyone in the Holy Spirit. Only Jesus has the power to baptize people with the actual Spirit of God. So we distinguish between Jesus' (and the Holy Spirit's) work of baptizing people in the Spirit and the church's work of baptizing people with water. As John said: "I baptize you with water for repentance, but he who is coming after me is mightier than I. . . . He will baptize you with the Holy Spirit and fire" (Matt. 3:11).

Because there is a difference between water baptism and Holy Spirit baptism, we may easily become confused and miss something important. Even though Spirit baptism is not the same thing as water baptism, one of the things that water baptism signifies is the baptism of the Holy Spirit. I am not saying that baptism conveys the baptism of the Holy Spirit or effects the baptism of the Holy Spirit; I'm saying that one of the things that baptism is a sign of is the baptism of the Holy Spirit. Baptism, like circumcision, is a sign of faith; it's not necessarily indicating the *presence* of faith, but it is the *sign* of faith. Circumcision was not faith, but it was the sign of Abraham's faith. In the New Testament, baptism is a *sign* of faith.

What baptism signifies, perhaps more than anything else as the sign of the covenant, is God's promise of redemption to all who are in Christ. That's why it is so multifaceted. The redemption that Christ accomplishes for His people includes and involves a cleansing from original sin; it includes regeneration; it includes justification; it includes sanctification; it includes resurrection and glorification. All the things that are constituent elements of the redemption that is wrought for us in Christ are signified by this covenant sign of baptism.

Does the sign necessarily bring to pass what is signified? Some churches believe in what is called *baptismal regeneration*. They believe that through the work of baptism, God the Holy Spirit gives not only the sign of regeneration but the *reality* of regeneration along with it. Historic Roman Catholic theology, for example, argues that the sacraments, including baptism, work *ex opere operato*—"through the working of the work." That is to say that the grace signified by baptism is conveyed through the actual working of the sacrament and that the sacrament, in a sense, automatically conveys to the recipient everything that the sign indicates. This has been a controversy chiefly between historic Roman Catholicism and Protestantism, but there are also debates on this point among Protestants. Some Protestant communions affirm that baptism regenerates *ex opere operato*, so that all who receive baptism receive spiritual rebirth and regeneration. The classic Reformed position does not share that viewpoint.

Another concern in the church is the validity of baptism. If you were baptized by a minister or a priest who then later repudiates the faith, is your baptism still valid? Do the baptism and its validity depend in any way on the integrity of the person who performs the rite? This was an issue during the *lapsi* and Donatist controversies in the early church. Through those controversies, the church concluded that three things are needed for a biblical baptism: form, matter, and intention. The form is to use the biblical Trinitarian formula in administering the sacrament: "In the name of the Father, the Son, and the Holy Spirit." The matter is the use of water. And the intention must be not simply to have someone get wet but to baptize and to be baptized according to the command of Christ (or, in the case of infant baptism, to present one's child for baptism according to the command of Christ). If these elements are present, then it is a valid baptism, regardless of the integrity of the one who administers the sign.

The reason for this is that baptism, as a sign of God's promise, depends for its validity not on the one who administers it or on the one who receives it but on the One whose promise it is, and that is God. This is why the church has often recognized the validity of baptisms that were performed even by heretics. Baptism is an important sign not because it is a sign of the promise of the church or the promise of the parent or the promise of the believer but because it is a sign of the promise of God Himself.

As noted above, Reformed theology does not see baptism as automatically conveying regeneration. Baptism points to the promise of God to save through faith in Christ, but it does not guarantee that salvation. In the Old Testament, some people who were circumcised were not automatically saved. That is, they had the sign of the promise of the old covenant, but they never inherited the actual promises behind that sign. The promises of God are mediated through faith, and we're still required to have faith in order to be redeemed.

Chapter Five

The Case against Infant Baptism

I n the next three chapters, we are going to turn our attention to perhaps the most controversial aspect of baptism: the proper recipients. Is it proper and appropriate to give this sacrament to infants, or is baptism to be administered only to those who have made a credible profession of faith? This is a debate in which many Christians who agree on everything else are not able to come to a unity of thinking. Before we get into this debate, I want to set the parameters for the discussion. Then, to the best of my ability, I will give the case *against* infant baptism and then the case *for* infant baptism. I personally hold to infant baptism, and I realize that it is hard to argue a position that you don't embrace yourself, but I will try to be as fair as I possibly can.

People on both sides of the issue want to be obedient to God and to the Word of God, and that's a good thing. The degree to which our children are involved in the life of the covenant community is not insignificant. How we worship God in the liturgy of the church is also not insignificant. We know how jealously God guarded the sanctity of worship in the Old Testament, and it is certainly the same God today who is concerned with how we worship Him. We must keep this in mind as we consider the subject of infant baptism.

One of the first issues we come across when considering infant baptism is that the New Testament does not give a direct, explicit command to baptize infants, whereas Old Testament Israel was explicitly commanded to circumcise infants. We don't have an explicit command in the New Testament to baptize infants, but we also don't have a prohibition on baptizing infants or an explicit command to baptize only professing believers. So whatever side one takes, it is important to acknowledge that each side must establish its case on the basis of inferences and implications drawn from Scripture. That kind of situation requires a measure of tolerance and forbearance for each other as we agree to disagree.

It also raises the question of what regulates our Christian behavior, particularly with respect to worship. Some communions argue that only things that God commands ought to be part of the liturgy of the church. Infant baptism is not commanded in Scripture, so it should not be part of the church's worship, the argument goes.

A second argument against infant baptism is that whatever else baptism signifies, it signifies faith; it is a sign of faith. When the Bible talks about baptizing people and gives a call to baptism, it will use such formulas as "Repent and be baptized" and "Believe and be baptized." Infants, it is argued, lack the ability to understand and respond to the gospel or to understand and confess sin. Since baptism is a sign of faith, why would you give a sign of faith to somebody who is not capable of having that faith?

A third argument against infant baptism is drawn from the historical narratives of the New Testament and the examples we find there. The book of Acts, for example, gives us the historical record of twelve baptisms. In every single one of those cases, the people who are mentioned as being baptized are adults. Not a single text in the New Testament explicitly teaches that infants were, in fact, baptized in the early church. Those who oppose infant baptism would certainly grant that in the Old Testament, we find both the explicit command to circumcise infants and the historical record of examples of infants who are circumcised. But we find neither of those in the New Testament when it comes to baptism.

A fourth argument against infant baptism stems from the extrabiblical historical record. An abundance of literature has survived from early in the history of the church, including the *Didache*, the letters of Clement, and the *Shepherd of Hermas*. We don't find a single reference to the baptism of an infant in any of the extrabiblical material until roughly the middle of the second century, which was more than a hundred years after the founding of Christianity. This leads many to conclude that the practice of infant baptism developed gradually in the life of the church through changes in its practices, and that these changes deviated from the Apostolic church of the first century.

A fifth argument against infant baptism is that the principle of ethnic or familial separation that operated in the Old Testament clearly does not operate in the New Testament. The principle of ethnic separation meant that the Jews were to keep themselves apart from the gentile community; they were not to be engaged in syncretistic cooperation with other religions or with gentiles. God had separated Israel to be a holy nation. The promises were to Abraham and to his seed, and the covenant promises were passed down through the line of biological descendants. We don't have that in the New Testament. The New Testament covenant is much more inclusive and expansive; God includes the principle of multiethnicity. That is, Greeks and Jews, Jews and gentiles, people from all families and tribes and tongues and nations, are incorporated in the new covenant community. It's not restricted in any way to one ethnic group or to one national group. So, the argument goes, the redemptive-historical change away from ethnic separation to a greater inclusiveness of ethnicity in the New Testament would do away with the giving of rites and rituals simply because a person is in a family relationship with a believer, as in the case of infant baptism.

We have seen that there is a link between Old Testament circumcision and New Testament baptism. Both function as covenant signs. Advocates of infant baptism appeal to the principle that the covenant sign in Israel was given to infant children of believers, so that because that tradition was established in the Old Testament, it is therefore to be continued in the New Testament. The case against infant baptism points out that though there are links between Old Testament circumcision and New Testament baptism, those links do not make the rites identical. There is both continuity and discontinuity between the new covenant and the old covenant. And there is no clear continuity with respect to the inclusion of infants in the giving of the covenant sign.

A sixth argument against infant baptism is that it is difficult, if not impossible or imprudent, to give the sign of baptism to infants in the way that the sign was first administered, which some argue was only by immersion. The argument is based on the Greek word *baptizō*, which, it is asserted, means "to dip" or "to immerse" rather than "to sprinkle." Therefore, if the baptism you received was not by immersion, then it was not a proper baptism. Baptism, it is argued, signifies dying and rising with Christ, and that meaning is more graphically demonstrated by immersion—by going under the water and coming back out of the water—than by pouring or sprinkling. It seems unsafe to immerse infants, so they must not be proper recipients of baptism.

Finally, a seventh argument against infant baptism is that the experience of baptism has much greater meaning to the person who experiences it as an adult than it does for an infant who is brought before a church and is sprinkled and doesn't even know what is going on. In terms of personal awareness and existential response to the sign, it is much more meaningful to receive it as an adult than as an infant.

I don't know where you stand on the issue of infant baptism, but it is important to be aware of why the people who differ from us hold the position they do. I used to teach the doctrine of the sacraments in a seminary where half the student body was Presbyterian and the other half was from a Baptist tradition. I had the unenviable task of teaching the sacraments to seniors, and I realized that if I persuaded my Baptist students of infant baptism, their whole ordination would be in jeopardy. I required the students who did not believe in infant baptism to write a paper on why other people *did* believe in infant baptism. Conversely, for those who believed in infant baptism, I required that they write a paper defending believer's baptism. I wanted them to be knowledgeable about the reasons that the debate exists. That's what I hope to accomplish in this brief study.

Chapter Six

The Case for Infant Baptism: Part 1

In the previous chapter, we briefly surveyed the chief arguments that are usually raised against the practice of infant baptism. Now we will turn to the reasons that certain churches practice infant baptism. It must first be noted that historically, the practice of infant baptism has been the overwhelming majority report in the history of the church. It is the practice of Rome, the practice of Eastern Orthodoxy, the practice of Episcopalianism, Methodism, Presbyterianism, Lutheranism, and so on. That does not make it valid, but it does mean that if that many Christians and Christian bodies historically have been convinced of infant baptism, then we ought to ask why so many embrace this practice if, indeed, the practice involves a departure from or distortion of the New Testament practice. Of course, you can't solve an issue of truth by counting noses.

The first argument against infant baptism was that there is no explicit command for it in the new covenant. We grant that, and then we reply that there is no explicit prohibition of it either. The case must be solved on other grounds and settled by inferences and implications. Our Baptist friends believe that the silence is a noisy one. They say that if God wanted the New Testament community to practice infant baptism, then He certainly wouldn't have remained silent about it. He would have made it explicit in the New Testament just as He did in the Old Testament regarding the practice of circumcision. Advocates of infant baptism say much the same thing: if God wanted to *discontinue* the practice of giving the sign of the covenant to the children of believers—previously circumcision, now baptism—then you would expect Him not to remain silent about this. He would explicitly correct that practice in the New Testament and state that there has been a change, that the sign of the covenant should no longer be given to the children of believers. Jewish converts to Christianity would have assumed that the principle of applying the covenant sign to children of believers would remain in effect unless countermanded by God, and God does not correct this assumption. Those who advocate for infant baptism see the silence of the New Testament as a point in favor of infant baptism rather than against it.

Second, advocates of believer's baptism and against infant baptism argue that, among other things, baptism is a sign of faith, and since children are not capable of having faith, baptism ought not to be administered to them. Advocates of infant baptism agree with the position of believer's baptism that circumcision is not identical to baptism but assert that the two rites nevertheless have an important point in common. Certainly, circumcision is a sign of faith, and this sign of faith in the old covenant was given to Abraham as an adult, after he professed faith. By divine mandate, it was given to Isaac, before Isaac exercised faith. It is clear, therefore, that one objection that will not stand is the objection that a sign of faith is improperly given to a human being before faith is present. If my Baptist friends object to infant baptism on the principle that it is improper to give the sign of faith to someone who does not have faith, then the argument proves too much. It proves that God was doing something wrong in the Old Testament when He most explicitly and emphatically did command that a sign of faith be given to infants.

An important point to understand here is that the substance to which the sign of the sacrament points is not necessarily tied to the moment that the sign is given. That which the sign signifies can come into effect after the sign is given, during the giving of the sign, or before the giving of the sign. In the case of circumcision in the Old Testament, Abraham believed and then received the sign of his faith, while Isaac received the sign of faith and then later came to faith. There were also those who received the sign of faith and never came to faith.

One thing we should mention at this point is that the debate between so-called infant baptism and believer's baptism focuses on the propriety of baptizing babies. Every church that practices infant baptism also practices adult baptism. Such churches require that for an unbaptized adult to be baptized, a profession of faith be given before the sign is given, because that is consistent with the practice of circumcision in the Old Testament. Someone who converted to Judaism as an adult in the Old Testament would have to give a profession of faith, an indication of credible repentance, before he could receive the sign as an adult. And that was also true in the New Testament community.

Third, the New Testament records twelve distinct cases of baptism, and in each of those cases, those who are listed as being baptized are adults. There is no explicit mention anywhere in the narrative history of the New Testament of an infant's being baptized. We may respond by saying that it is true that all the baptisms recorded in Acts are of adults, and that those adults profess faith before they are baptized. This is consistent with the point that we agree on: in the case of believer's baptism, there must be a prior profession of faith. In three of the twelve examples recorded in the New Testament, however (25 percent of them), there is reference to what is called *household baptism*. In those cases, the individual *and the household* are baptized. This brings to mind the occasion when Paul and Silas spoke to the Philippian jailer, who asked, "What must I do to be saved?" They answered, "Believe in the Lord Jesus, and you will be saved, you and your household" (Acts 16:30–31). Does the term "household" necessarily include infants? I would say no, it doesn't. We know many people who have households that do not include infants. But in terms of the use of the English word "household," may it include infants? Certainly it may.

When I say, "My wife and family," that communicates that my wife and I have children. It doesn't say how old they are, but it does say that we have children. Oscar Cullmann, a leading New Testament scholar and theologian of the twentieth century, did an exhaustive study of the word *oikos*, which is the Greek word that is translated as "house" or "household." He argued that *oikos* is not ambiguous, but that it has specific reference to infants. If he's right, that would settle the debate once and for all.

Cullmann's conclusion with respect to "infants" specifically being meant when the word *oikos* is used is probably a stretch, but even if *oikos* refers only to children rather than infants, it would be an important point. It would mean that there is continuity from the Old Testament to the New Testament when it comes to the principle of familial incorporation into the covenant by way of the covenant sign. The reason that children were given circumcision as a sign in the old covenant is that they were part of the household of adult believers, and we see a carryover in the book of Acts of this familial solidarity with respect to baptism.

An even more compelling point about these examples in the New Testament is that when we read about the people who were baptized, there is no evidence that any of them were children of Christian believers at the time of their infancy. They were first-generation believers; most if not all came from the gentile world and would not have been children of Christian parents. In other words, if we had an example in the New Testament of somebody's being baptized as an adult who we knew was a child of Christian believers at the time of his infancy and had not been baptized as an infant, then that would have some significance to his being baptized as an adult. It would indicate that there was a practice of restricting baptism to adults and excluding the infant children of believers. But we do not have such an example. Remember, both sides believe in the principle of adult baptism. Examples of adult converts who are baptized on profession of faith do not then invalidate infant baptism. So in terms of examples, the New Testament evidence favors infant baptism rather than working against it.

Fourth, there is the record of church history that we referred to in chapter 5. In the literature that survives from the early church, the first reference to infant baptism that we can find is from the middle of the second century. Let's say that it was approximately the year 150. This is the inference that some people draw from that: "This must indicate that the practice of infant baptism began a hundred years or so after the inauguration of the Christian church. And it took that long for the departure from orthodoxy to occur." This historical reference is one of the most convincing arguments *for* infant baptism. Why? Because the reference we have to infant baptism in the middle of the second century refers in passing to infant baptism as the universal practice of the church. It is not simply a report of an isolated case of infant baptism, but it is a comment on the universal practice.

One would have to say that this departure from the pristine purity of the Apostolic age took place rapidly enough to infiltrate the whole Christian world in approximately seventy-five to a hundred years, and it did so without a single word of theological debate surviving in the literature from the period. Now, the literature that survived from the first and second centuries is replete with references to the doctrinal disputes of the day. Is it plausible that if the New Testament community did not practice infant baptism and a later generation instituted this deviation from the New Testament practice, there would have been no debate about it? It is possible that there was a fierce debate about it and that whatever literature was involved in that debate has simply passed from the scene. The odds of that happening, however, are astronomical.

The record indicates that it was actually *opposition* to infant baptism that was a late occurrence in the church. This opposition came into vogue as part of the protest against sacramentalism, which teaches that baptism automatically converts or automatically puts recipients into a state of grace. People reacted against that and said, "If people think they're saved simply because they're baptized, we'd better stop this practice of baptizing infants, because they're coming to the same false conclusions that the Jews came to in the Old Testament." (But we should note that those false conclusions did not lead the prophets of Israel to discontinue the practice of infant circumcision.)

As we continue our discussion of baptism in the next chapter, let me say that it is worth the struggle to understand this issue, because what we're debating and discussing has to do with how we can most honor God and how we can most be faithful to the application of His promises and of His signs to His people. Often in theology, we have a tendency to embrace, adopt, and defend theological views not because we've carefully searched them out as the Bereans did in the New Testament but because of our history and traditions. Those things are important, but let us always strive for fidelity to God and to His Word and to be instructed by the Scriptures in these difficult questions of differences of opinion.

Chapter Seven

The Case for Infant Baptism: Part 2

In chapter 6, we examined some key arguments for infant baptism. Now I want to respond to one of the chief objections to infant baptism, which we saw as the fifth argument—namely, that the principle of ethnic separation established in the Old Testament, by which God separated unto Himself a particular nation as a chosen people, is discontinued in the New Testament. And since redemption is not carried out through a particular people in the New Testament, there is no reason to continue the idea of ethnic separation such as was found in the Old Testament. Certainly the New Testament makes it clear that the gospel is given to all nations and that gentiles and Samaritans and all who believe in Christ are invited to full participation in the New Testament covenant.

First, we need to understand that the Old Testament did not teach that ethnic separation guaranteed salvation. Paul tells us:

> For circumcision indeed is of value if you obey the law, but if you break the law, your circumcision becomes uncircumcision. So, if a man who is uncircumcised keeps the precepts of the law, will not his uncircumcision be regarded as circumcision? Then he who is physically uncircumcised but keeps the law will condemn you who have the written code and circumcision but break the law. For no one is a Jew who is merely one outwardly, nor is circumcision outward and physical. But a Jew is one inwardly, and circumcision is a matter of the heart, by the Spirit, not by the letter. His praise is not from man but from God. (Rom. 2:25–29)

Paul is arguing against a view commonly held among the Pharisees that because they were the physical descendants of Abraham, they were redeemed; they didn't need repentance as displayed in the baptism of John. Some assumed that because they were circumcised, they were therefore saved. But that idea was negated by the prophets in the Old Testament who talked about the remnant who would be saved and the children of promise who would be saved, and that not all the descendants of Abraham would, in fact, be saved. Paul makes it abundantly clear that even among the Jews, circumcision did not guarantee redemption. Yes, to be sure, the nation was set apart to be a light to the gentiles, but that consecration of Israel for its task did not carry with it the implication that everyone who was a part of that nation would, in fact, be saved.

Of course, the same problem arises with respect to baptism. Some believe that baptism in itself saves; the same error that occurred in the Old Testament with respect to circumcision is often repeated by Christians today. New Testament baptism is the sign of the covenant of God's promise, but the content of that promise rests on the exercise of faith, just as in the old covenant the content of the promise signified by circumcision rested on the exercise of faith. Since that's the case, we may ask, What, then, was the value of circumcision if it didn't save? If it didn't guarantee redemption, what good was it? Paul raises that question when he asks: "Then what advantage has the Jew? Or what is the value of circumcision?" (Rom. 3:1). He answers: "Much in every way. To begin with, the Jews were entrusted with the oracles of God. What if some were unfaithful? Does their faithlessness nullify the faithfulness of God?" (vv. 2–3). Paul answers his own question emphatically: "By no means! Let God be true though every one were a liar" (v. 4).

Paul makes it clear that circumcision did not guarantee salvation, and then he asks, "What advantage is it?" We might expect him to say that it is of no advantage, but instead he states that there was a great advantage to being a Jew because the Jews had been given the oracles of God. They had been given the Word of God. And part of that Word, if you will, was circumcision. Circumcision was the visible manifestation and confirmation of the promise of God. In effect, Paul is asking, "What advantage is it for a person to have the promise of God, a promise that is given to all who believe?" And he argues that it is an enormous advantage to know and to receive the promise of God, and that even if men break the promise, the faithfulness of God remains intact.

This is extremely important for us in understanding baptism in the New Testament. Again, baptism is not identical to circumcision, but circumcision and baptism have this in common: they are both signs of God's covenant of promise, the promise given to all who believe. The signs don't automatically transmit the content of the promise; faith is still required, but what is automatically conveyed by the sign is the promise of God for all who believe. In the Old Testament, circumcision was a sign of faith. Abraham was to receive the sign after he expressed his faith. But his infant son Isaac received the sign of faith before he had faith. Of whose faith was circumcision a sign with Isaac? Similarly, when infants are baptized, whose faith is being signified? Often when I ask that question of people who practice infant baptism, they say, "Well, it's a sign of the faith of the parents." I say no; it's because of the faith of one parent that the child is eligible to receive the sign, but it is a sign of the child's faith—though the child may not yet possess that faith—and it is the sign of God's promise to all who subsequently come to faith.

During the Reformation, the Anabaptist controversy arose among Protestants. The prefix *ana-* means "again," so Anabaptism refers to being baptized again or a second time. The Anabaptists in the sixteenth century refused to recognize Roman Catholic baptism, so they baptized Protestant converts again. Similarly, modern baptistic churches, when people who were baptized as infants want to become members, may require rebaptism. Yet to those churches, it's not really a second baptism but rather the first baptism, because they don't believe that the first baptism was valid.

Many people who have been baptized as infants come to faith later in life. Many times, such people have said to me: "I was baptized as an infant, and it didn't mean a thing to me. Would you please baptize me as an adult, now that I understand what it's all about?" I tell them that I cannot do that, for two reasons. First, it is against the theological standards of my denomination, and second, I don't believe in doing it, because I believe that I would be sinning against God to baptize someone a second time. I also think the person would be sinning against God to be baptized a second time.

This can create quite a reaction. People usually want to experience the existential import of baptism. They want it to be "meaningful," but baptism is the sign of God's promise of all the things accompanying redemption. If you received the sign of His promise as an infant and later in life came to faith, then when you came to faith, all that your baptism signified was given to you in reality. Would you then go to God and say: "God, would You run it by me again? I didn't really have confidence in the trustworthiness of Your promise the first time, and so now that You've fulfilled Your promise, would You make that promise to me again?" That would be insulting to the integrity of God.

A key text for thinking about infant baptism is 1 Corinthians 7:12–14. In verses 12–13, Paul writes: "To the rest I say (I, not the Lord) that if any brother has a wife who is an unbeliever, and she consents to live with him, he should not divorce her. If any woman has a husband who is an unbeliever, and he consents to live with her, she should not divorce him." This is part of Paul's instruction about marriage between a believer and an unbeliever, presupposing that they were both unbelievers at the time of their union, but the salient portion of this text for our concern is verse 14: "For the unbelieving husband is made holy because of his wife, and the unbelieving wife is made holy because of her husband. Otherwise your children would be unclean, but as it is, they are holy."

This is a tough text because Paul states that the unbelieving wife is "made holy" by the believing husband and vice versa, and we normally think of being made "holy"—or "sanctified" in other translations—as a process that is subsequent to our justification. We say that we are justified and *then* we begin the process of sanctification, so it would seem that if people who are unbelievers are holy, it must mean that they are also justified. Does this mean that there are two ways of justification, one by faith and the other by marriage? If you yourself do not believe, then just marry somebody who does, and you're redeemed? This is not what Paul means here; rather, he uses the term "holy" in the classic Jewish religious sense.

The primary meaning of "holy" is "consecrated" or "set apart." In the Old Testament, to be sanctified or consecrated meant that you could participate in the life of the covenant people of God. Paul gives this teaching of the consecration of the unbelieving spouse with the specific view toward the status of any children that come from this union. The reason that the unbelieving husband is "made holy" by the believing wife or the unbelieving wife "made holy" by the believing husband is so that their children may not be unclean. For now "they are holy." Children born of a union that includes at least one believer are considered holy and not unclean.

In Jewish speech, the term *unclean* is filled with covenantal significance. Being unclean meant being a stranger to the covenant, outside the camp, a foreigner and an alien to the community of the people of God. Here, Paul clearly placed infants within the context of the covenant community, for now they are holy. That is, they are set apart; they are consecrated. I think that's one of the main reasons that many baptistic churches nevertheless practice infant dedication, which I remind my friends is an Old Testament rite, not a New Testament rite. The concept of dedication came in the Old Testament. It was connected with purification rites and with circumcision. But the reason that children are dedicated is that the church universal understands that infants do have a special place in the life of the church. They are to be considered part of the covenant community because they are not unclean; they are holy. So this is the only question left to ask at this point: If they are part of the covenant community, why would you withhold from them the sign of the covenant, the sign of their consecration, the sign of their cleanliness, and the sign of their being holy?

The sixth argument against infant baptism is that the Greek term *baptizō*—from which we get the English "to baptize"—must involve and mean immersion. Leviticus 14 provides instructions for purification rites for those who have been cleansed of leprosy or declared by the priest to be free of leprosy. One of the rites involves taking two birds; one bird is killed, and the blood from that bird is drained into a basin. The second bird is then dipped into the blood of the first bird. Obviously, there would not be enough blood in the first bird so that the second bird could be immersed in it. What is significant is that the Greek word used in the ancient Greek translation of Leviticus is *baptizō*. So we have there a specific use of the Greek term *baptizō* that does not mean "immersion." Based on other texts such as Mark 7:4, which speaks of "the washing [literally, 'baptizing'] of cups and pots and copper vessels and dining couches," we ought to understand that *baptizō* does not necessarily always mean "to immerse" but instead refers to ceremonial washing that can easily be accomplished by sprinkling or pouring. For how would someone immerse a couch?

The seventh objection to infant baptism has to do with one's subjective experience of baptism and one's personal apprehension of its meaning. Perhaps you have struggled with your baptism and wondered about it because it didn't mean a whole lot to you when you were a child. Or perhaps you were baptized by a clergyman who later turned out to be a scoundrel or a heretic. Maybe something has made you uncomfortable about your status in the presence of God related to your baptism. Let me assure you that the single most important point to remember about baptism is that it is a sign of the promise of God and that its validity depends not on the person who receives it or the person who administers it but on the person whose sacred promise it is. Though every man "were a liar," the Apostle Paul insists, God is faithful (Rom. 3:4), and if He has marked you with this sign, then you bear an indelible mark on your soul indicating that God has given His promise. He doesn't need to swear that promise more than once. Though we do repeat other ordinances, such as the Lord's Supper, for continued strength, baptism is a one-time experience. Circumcision occurred once. God's covenant with Abraham was made once. Once God swore by Himself that He would keep the terms of the covenant,

He was not subjected to repeated experiences of it. With our baptism—it is intended to be a one-time experience by which the person is marked forever with the promise of God. This is a great advantage to the troubled conscience.

Chapter Eight

The Body of Christ

We have seen in our study of the sacraments that there is great disagreement about baptism, but those differences pale in comparison to the disunity that exists concerning the Lord's Supper. One of the tragedies of the sixteenth-century Protestant Reformation was that the unity that existed initially among the Reformers was quickly broken, chiefly over a difference of understanding of the Lord's Supper. Martin Luther and the Lutherans in Germany did not agree with the Reformed in Switzerland about the meaning and function of the Lord's Supper. And among the Swiss Reformers, there was debate and division over the Lord's Supper. Even in Switzerland, two of the leading Reformers, Huldrych Zwingli and John Calvin, differed sharply in their understanding of the Lord's Supper. Many of those differences have persisted to this day. On the one hand, we have a difference between Protestants and Roman Catholics, and on the other hand, there are differences among Protestants. So to begin our study of the Lord's Supper, we will look at the classical Roman Catholic view of the sacrament.

The term that defines the Roman Catholic view of the Lord's Supper is *transubstantiation*. This term is rooted not only in Roman Catholic history but also in the function of theology, where theology was greatly influenced by philosophical categories that have their roots in Aristotle. Aristotle made a distinction with respect to *being* or *substance*. He distinguished not only between form and matter but also between the *substance* of an object and its *accidens*.

According to Aristotle, the substance of an object is that which a thing is in its deepest essence; the *accidens* of a thing is what we would define as the external, perceivable qualities of the thing—that which meets the eye. The color, texture, and shape of something all have to do with external qualities that we perceive on the surface. We know, for example, from modern science that things are made up of atoms and subatomic particles and molecules and cells. But when I look at a person, I don't see atoms and neutrons and protons; I see somebody who is tall or short and old or young. I'm looking at the external, perceivable qualities.

This is important for trying to understand transubstantiation, because the Roman Catholic Church made use of some of these philosophical categories to articulate its view of the sacrament. Rome believes that in the celebration of the Mass or the Lord's Supper, a supernatural—indeed, miraculous—event takes place. At the time of the prayer of consecration, the common elements of bread and wine undergo a transformation—a *transubstantiation*. The substance of the bread and wine is changed into the substance of the body and blood of Christ. At the same time, the *accidens* remains the same.

What you have after the prayer of consecration is the real substance of the body and blood of Jesus. The substance of the bread and the wine has disappeared, yet those elements still look like bread and wine, they taste like bread and wine, they smell like bread and wine, they feel like bread and wine, and if you were to drop them on the floor, they would sound like bread and wine. But they are not bread and wine; they are the real body and blood of Jesus.

This is why, for example, when Roman Catholic parishioners enter the sanctuary and are about to enter the pew, they kneel or genuflect. As the priest is working at the altar, he will at certain moments cross himself or bow or genuflect. He's doing that with a view to something specific: he is giving veneration toward the tabernacle. The tabernacle is a little box, often made of gold, that is atop the altar in the center front of the church, and in the tabernacle is the host—that is, the bread that is consecrated and transubstantiated into the body of Christ. So people are bowing not before the altar but before Christ, since He is believed to be truly present in the consecrated host.

It's important to understand that disagreement between Protestants and Roman Catholics over transubstantiation is not simply a disagreement over the question of sacrament. Essentially, the issue has to do with our understanding of Christology. It is a Christological dispute, and it has to do with our understanding of the human nature of Jesus. For example, if transubstantiation is true and if the Mass is celebrated on the same day in Poland, in Alaska, in California, in France, in Southeast Asia, and in Africa all at the same time, and the real flesh and blood of Jesus is present in all these places at the same time, it would require the body of Jesus, which belongs properly to His humanity and not to His deity, to be present all over the globe at the same time. That is, the human nature of Jesus would require the power of ubiquity or omnipresence.

When understanding the person of Christ, the church has always had to struggle to understand the mystery of the incarnation in such a way that we confess the true deity of Christ as well as His true humanity. The Council of Chalcedon in 451 defined the dual nature of Christ in these terms: Christ is *vere homo, vere Deus*—"truly man, truly God." Arguing against the heretics of the fifth century, the Monophysites and the Nestorians, Chalcedon affirmed that the two natures of Christ are perfectly united. Then it stated four distinct negatives. The two natures are without mixture, confusion, separation, or division. That is, the two natures of Jesus cannot be blended together so that you have one nature that's neither really God nor man; nor can they be torn asunder so that the unity is broken into two separate persons. The last statement of the Chalcedon formula is this: each nature retains its own attributes. That is, historic orthodox Christianity states that in the incarnation, the attributes of humanity remain with the human nature and the attributes of deity remain with the divine nature. So for Jesus' body to be everywhere present would require Jesus' human nature to have a divine attribute.

Historically, Rome has answered this in a somewhat complicated way based on its understanding of what is called the *communication of attributes*. Rome says that the attribute of omnipresence, which belongs to the divine nature, is communicated to or shared with the human nature so that now according to His human nature Christ can be in more than one place at the same time. The Reformers objected strongly to transubstantiation on this very point because they saw in this teaching a violation of the Council of Chalcedon and a confusing of the two natures of Christ. They saw a thinly veiled form of the old Monophysite tendency to deify the human nature of Christ.

For the most part, the Reformers rejected the idea of the omnipresence of Jesus' human nature. There was one very notable exception: Martin Luther. Luther rejected transubstantiation, but he argued for the physical, corporeal presence of the body of Jesus in the Lord's Supper. He agreed with Rome's understanding of the communication of attributes, so he did not break as seriously from Rome as the other Reformers did. At one discussion of the Lord's Supper, Luther kept repeating the words that came from the Mass and from the New Testament: *Hoc est corpus meum*—"This is My body." At the institution of the Lord's Supper, Jesus said "This is My body" when He picked up the bread. He didn't say, "This represents My body." He said, "This is My body." Luther insisted that Jesus meant what He said. Though Luther rejected the Aristotelian formula of transubstantiation, he argued that the body and blood of Jesus are truly, corporeally present in, under, and with the elements of bread and wine.

Whatever your view is on transubstantiation, it is important for us as Christians to study as deeply as we can the significance of the Lord's Supper because it represents an important part of the life of the people of God and of the liturgy of the church. Virtually every church has some practice and celebration of the Lord's Supper. Too often it is an outward ritual that we don't think much about, and that is to our own great loss. In my own life, it's been a benefit for me to be a professional theologian and to be able to spend more time studying these things than most other Christians ever have the opportunity to do. One of the great benefits is that the more I study the Lord's Supper, the richer it is for my Christian experience and the more it moves me to a depth of worship in the life of the church. Whatever your position is on this point, give it the benefit of a second glance and begin to study it. This is one of the doctrines and mysteries we will never exhaust, in terms of our understanding, during our Christian lives.

Chapter Nine

The Present Aspect of Christ's Presence

I once rode a bus through a depressed area of a mill city near Pittsburgh, after the mills had been shut down. There was a high level of unemployment there, and I noticed that many stores were boarded up. It was a bleak winter day, and the snow along the sides of the streets had turned to dark colors because of the soot and cinders. People were cold. They would get on the bus, and I could see a sense of despair etched in their faces. It was so gloomy that I asked myself, "Is there any hope for these people?"

As I was asking this very question, I noticed a storefront church with the sign of the cross in the window. I smiled to myself and thought, "There's their sign of hope." A little farther down the street I saw another church, and then another church, and I soon discovered that I couldn't go for more than a city block without somewhere seeing the sign of the cross—the sign of the greatest hope of mankind. I thought, "You know, as I'm sitting here on this bus, somewhere in the world at this very moment, people are gathered together around a table, celebrating the death of Christ." I don't think a second ticks on the clock when there isn't someone somewhere on this planet engaged in remembering the death of Christ. It has been seared into our minds, as Christ intended.

When Christ instituted the sacrament of the Lord's Supper in the upper room with His disciples, He said, "Do this in remembrance of me" (Luke 22:19). Memory has to do with holding in one's mind the thought of something that has taken place in the past. The Lord's Supper involves the people of God's corporate experience of remembering what Jesus has accomplished in the *past*. But not only is there this past reference, there is also the *future* reference. Jesus said that He wanted to celebrate the Passover with

His friends one last time before He would celebrate it with them in His Father's house in heaven (see vv. 15–16). Paul wrote, "For as often as you eat this bread and drink the cup, you proclaim the Lord's death until he comes" (1 Cor. 11:26). There is a sense that when we celebrate the Lord's Supper, we don't just look to the past to what's already been accomplished with the death of Christ, but we also look forward to the glorious future, when God promises to have a wedding banquet in heaven for the Son and His bride, the church. We look for the great banquet feast, and we have a down payment, a foretaste of that future glory, every time we assemble to celebrate the Lord's Supper.

Most of the controversy with respect to the Lord's Supper has to do with the *present*. What is the present significance of this sacrament? Closely related to that question of the present is the question of *presence*. Does the church believe in the real presence of Christ at the Lord's Supper? This was one of the questions debated during the sixteenth century. Rome insisted then and does still now insist that Christ is truly, corporeally present in the elements of the supper by virtue of transubstantiation. Luther also argued for the real presence of Christ in the Lord's Supper in a corporeal way, though not through the elements' being transformed into the body and blood of Christ. Then there was the debate between the Lutherans and the Reformed, and the intramural debate among the Reformed, between Huldrych Zwingli and John Calvin.

Zwingli took the position that the Lord's Supper is a symbol, and so Christ is only symbolically present in the Lord's Supper. Zwingli believed that the Lord's Supper is essentially a memorial; it is a sign of the past and a sign of the future. It is a sign of Christ's presence now in the sense that God is present everywhere. But Zwingli argued that Christ has no real *presence* in the Lord's Supper; the supper is merely a memorial. The majority of evangelical Protestants today hold this memorial view of the Lord's Supper.

This was not, however, Luther's view, and it certainly was not Calvin's view. In fact, one of the interesting footnotes to the debate in the sixteenth century was Calvin's use of the word *substance*. Whenever he debated with the Lutherans about the presence of Christ in the sacrament, Calvin would not use the word *substance*. When he argued with the Zwinglians, however, he insisted on using the term *substance*. Was this because Calvin was inconsistent? Not at all. He was fighting a two-front war, and he understood that the term *substance* can be used in more than one way. Sometimes the word *substance* is a synonym for "physical presence." To say that something is *substantially* there is to say that it is physically there. That was Luther's view, and that was Rome's view. So when Calvin was arguing with them, he wouldn't use the word *substance*. But the term *substance* can also mean "real"—that is, not imagined or symbolic. So when Calvin argued with Zwingli, he insisted on the substantial presence of Christ—not in the sense of "physical" but rather in the sense of "real." So the Reformed community in the sixteenth century strongly affirmed the real presence of Christ, which was then carried on in Reformed churches, Presbyterian churches, and the Anglican Church.

Calvin's view requires some thinking related to the mystery of the incarnation. We believe that Jesus Christ is one person with two natures. He has a divine nature and a human nature. The human nature includes His body, which can be at only one place at one time. It is subject to the normal limitations of physical forms; there is an outline to His body. There is a certain sense that Jesus, according to His human nature, as the Reformed confessions tell us, is no longer with us; He's no longer present. Jesus told His disciples before He departed by way of the ascension, "A little while, and you will see me no longer" (John 16:16). He was going away. He talked about His departure, the removal of His physical presence from their midst. And ever since His ascension, the church has looked forward to the day of His bodily return, when He will appear once again and every eye will see Him.

Yet Jesus also said, "Behold, I am with you always, to the end of the age" (Matt. 28:20). How can He be present and absent at the same time? In this case, a person can be present and absent at the same time but not in the same relationship. According to His human nature, Jesus is no longer present with us; according to His divine nature, He is never absent from us. The one person of Christ is omnipresent thanks to His divine nature, so Jesus can be in Alaska and South America and Pennsylvania and Eastern Europe and East Asia and Africa all at the same time. His body can't be in all these places at the same time because His body belongs to His human nature. The divine nature is real, so when the person of Christ is present according to His divine nature, He is really present. This was the point that Calvin insisted on.

Our Lutheran friends ask: "Are you saying that there's a place where the divine nature is present but the human nature isn't? Aren't you dividing and separating the two natures? Aren't you doing the very thing that Chalcedon condemned Nestorians for doing in the fifth century?" No. The one person of Christ has two natures: a human nature and a divine nature. Those two natures can be distinguished from each other, but they must not be separated. There is a big difference between *distinguishing* between the two natures and *dividing* the two natures. I can distinguish your body and soul and do you no harm; if I divide them, I've just killed you.

Now, we have one person, Jesus Christ. His human nature does not have the attribute of omnipresence, so according to His human nature, Christ is localized; He is at the right hand of God. He is in heaven, wherever that is, and He cannot be in five different places at the same time according to His human nature. But Christ's divine nature does have the attribute of omnipresence; it is not subject to the physical or geographical limits that the human nature is. If this were not the case, during the incarnation, God would have been limited to the body of Jesus and would have been nowhere else. God can never stop being eternal, spiritual, immutable, and omnipresent, even when God the Son takes to Himself a human nature. So according to

His divine nature, Christ can be in Paris and London and Orlando all at the same time.

When we go to the Lord's Supper, are we communing with Christ only according to His divine nature? No, for while according to His human nature Christ is in heaven, according to His divine nature He is everywhere. His human and divine natures are perfectly united, so as I commune with Him according to His divine nature in the supper, I commune with the whole Christ. Calvin said that in a mystical way the human nature is made present to me, not because the human nature comes down from heaven but because when I enter into communion with the one person of Christ, and in the person of Christ the divine and human natures are perfectly united, then mystically I am brought into the presence of the resurrected Christ. I am mystically entering heaven itself, where our sanctuary is. So I am not cut off from Christ according to His human nature. When I take the Lord's Supper, I am communing with the whole Christ.

This was Calvin's explanation, and Luther found it amazing. Philip Melanchthon referred to Calvin as "the theologian," because he articulated this explanation such that the people of God had an understanding of real presence, real communion, without violating the concepts of the Council of Chalcedon, without deifying the human nature of Jesus and making it locally present in manifold places.

Christ is, of course, present in every worship service. But something special, something mystical, happens when we gather and partake of the Lord's Supper and feast on the whole Christ. This is a special meeting that Christ has ordained between Himself and His people, whereupon He spreads His table for us.

There is great human significance to that. I like to tell the Old Testament story of Mephibosheth (2 Sam. 9). He was the lone survivor of the household of Saul, and he was lame in both feet. King David sought him out and brought Mephibosheth to the royal palace. For the sake of David's love for Jonathan, David gave Mephibosheth full membership in his family, and he gave him the unspeakable privilege of dining at the king's table every day. Table fellowship is significant. When we have a person into our home and spread our table for that person as a guest, a special kind of communion takes place over a meal, and Jesus invites His people not only to be in His presence but to come to His table.

The biggest difficulty in living the Christian life is believing in, worshiping, serving, and seeking to obey a God who is invisible to us. So often our Christian lives are defined by a profound sense of the absence of God. This is one of the reasons that I love the Lord's Supper. God, through this sacrament, manifests His presence with outward signs that guarantee His promise to be with us, to heal us, to forgive us, to strengthen us. At no time in my spiritual life am I more acutely aware of the reality of the presence of Christ than in the sacrament of the Lord's Supper. Coming in that moment, for that drama, and remembering Christ's promise to His people that He would be there and that He would be the Bread of Life that comes down to us from heaven thrills my soul.

About the Author

Dr. R.C. Sproul was the founder of Ligonier Ministries, founding pastor of Saint Andrew's Chapel in Sanford, Fla., first president of Reformation Bible College, and executive editor of *Tabletalk* magazine. His radio program, *Renewing Your Mind*, is still broadcast daily on hundreds of radio stations around the world and can also be heard online. He was the author of more than one hundred books, including *The Holiness of God*, *Chosen by God*, and *Everyone's a Theologian*. He was recognized throughout the world for his articulate defense of the inerrancy of Scripture and the need for God's people to stand with conviction upon His Word.

Free eBooks *by* R.C. Sproul

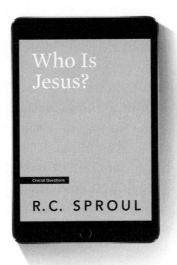

Does prayer really change things? Can I be sure I'm saved? Dr. R.C. Sproul answers these important questions, along with more than forty others, in his Crucial Questions series. Designed for the Christian or thoughtful inquirer, these booklets can be used for personal study, small groups, and conversations with family and friends. Browse the collection and download your free digital ebooks today.

Get 3 free months of *Tabletalk.*

In 1977, R.C. Sproul started *Tabletalk* magazine.
Today it has become the most widely read subscriber-based monthly
devotional magazine in the world. **Try it free for 3 months.**

TryTabletalk.com/CQ | 800-435-4343

ASK LIGONIER

Do we have free will?

Is it true that God controls everything?

Does prayer change things?

A Place to Find Answers

Maybe you're leading a Bible study tomorrow. Maybe you're just beginning to dig deeper. It's good to know that you can always ask Ligonier. For more than fifty years, Christians have been looking to Ligonier Ministries, the teaching fellowship of R.C. Sproul, for clear and helpful answers to biblical and theological questions. Now you can ask those questions online as they arise, confident that our team will work quickly to provide clear, concise, and trustworthy answers. The *Ask Ligonier* podcast provides another avenue for you to submit questions to some of the most trusted pastors and teachers who are serving the church today. When you have questions, just ask Ligonier.

FOR MORE INFORMATION, VISIT ASK.LIGONIER.ORG